# What Has Wheels



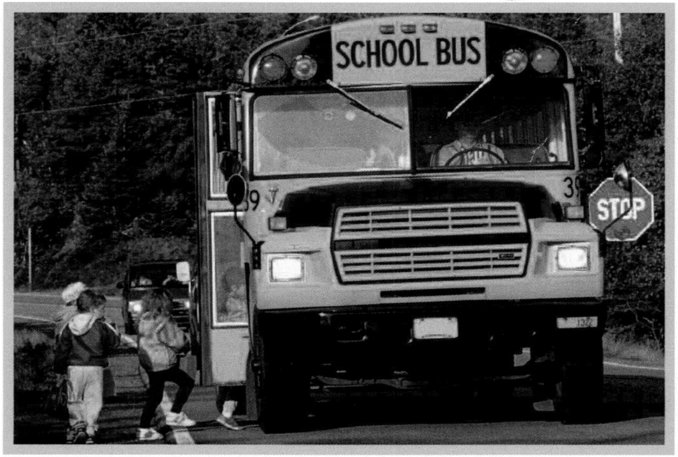


written by Karen Hoenecke

KAEDEN BOOKS™

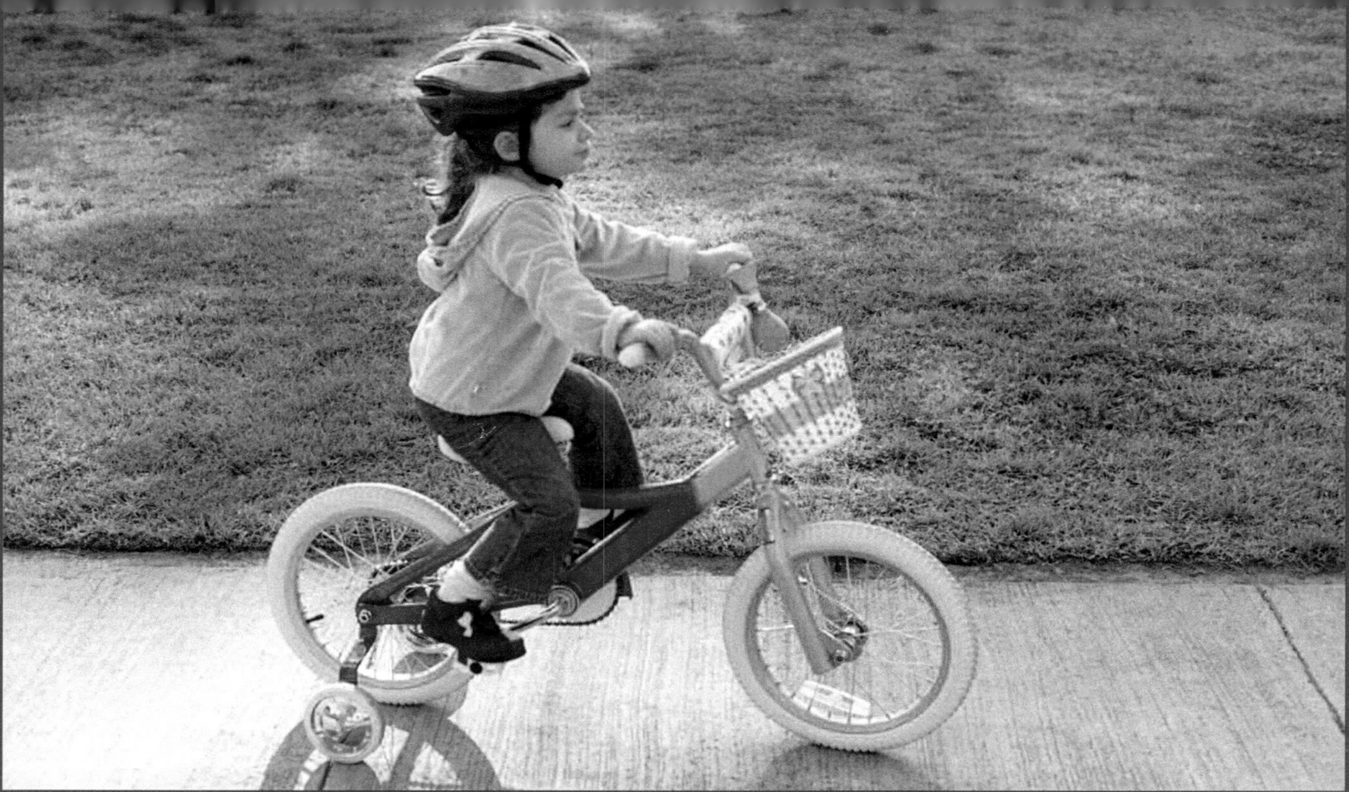

A bike has wheels.

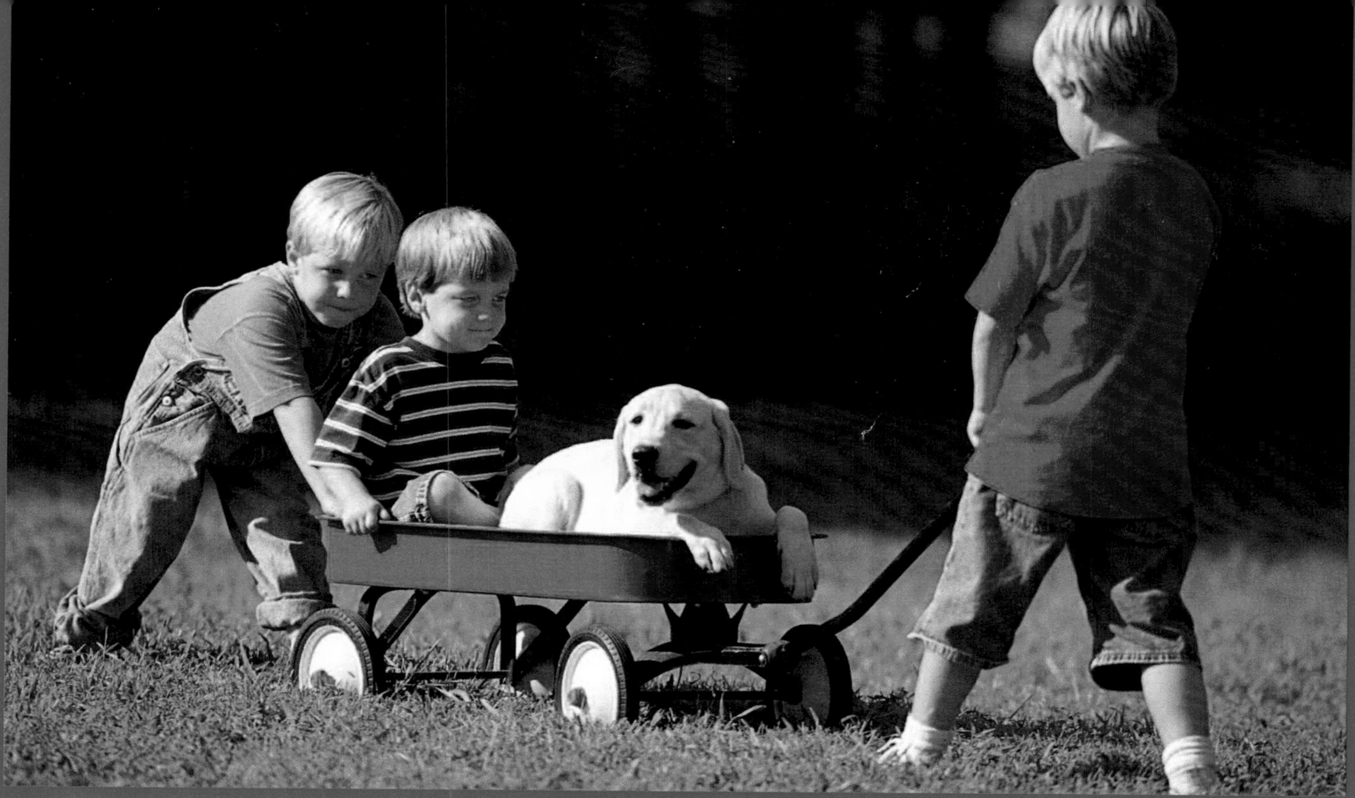

A wagon has wheels.

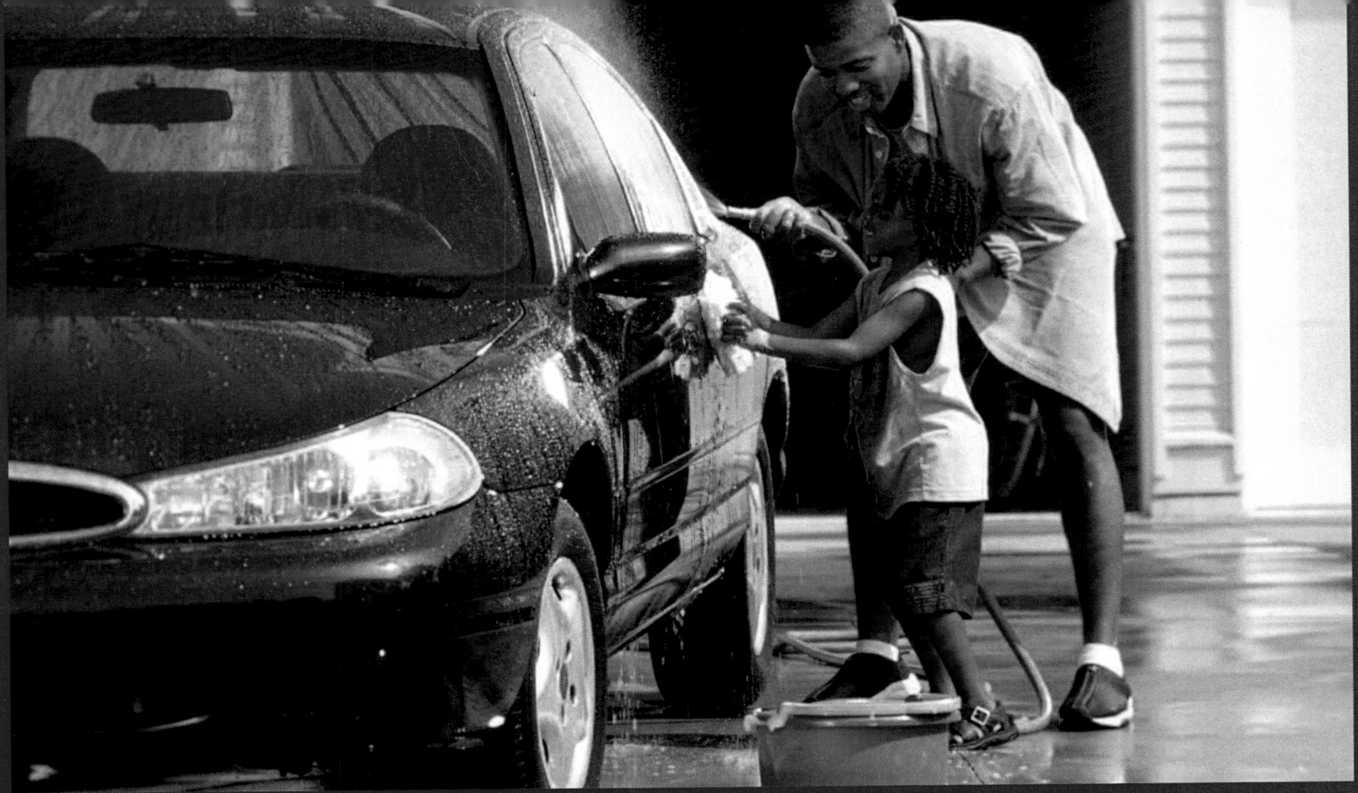

A car has wheels.

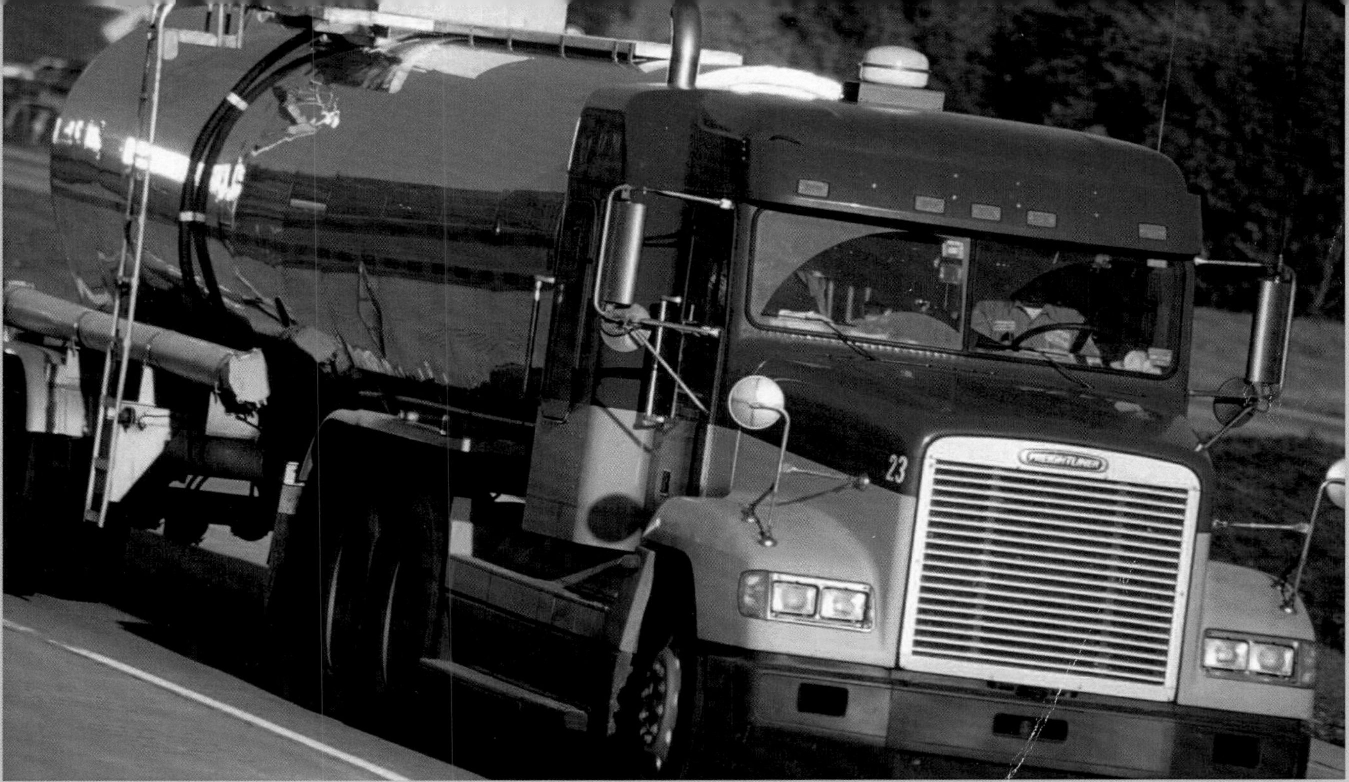

A truck has wheels.

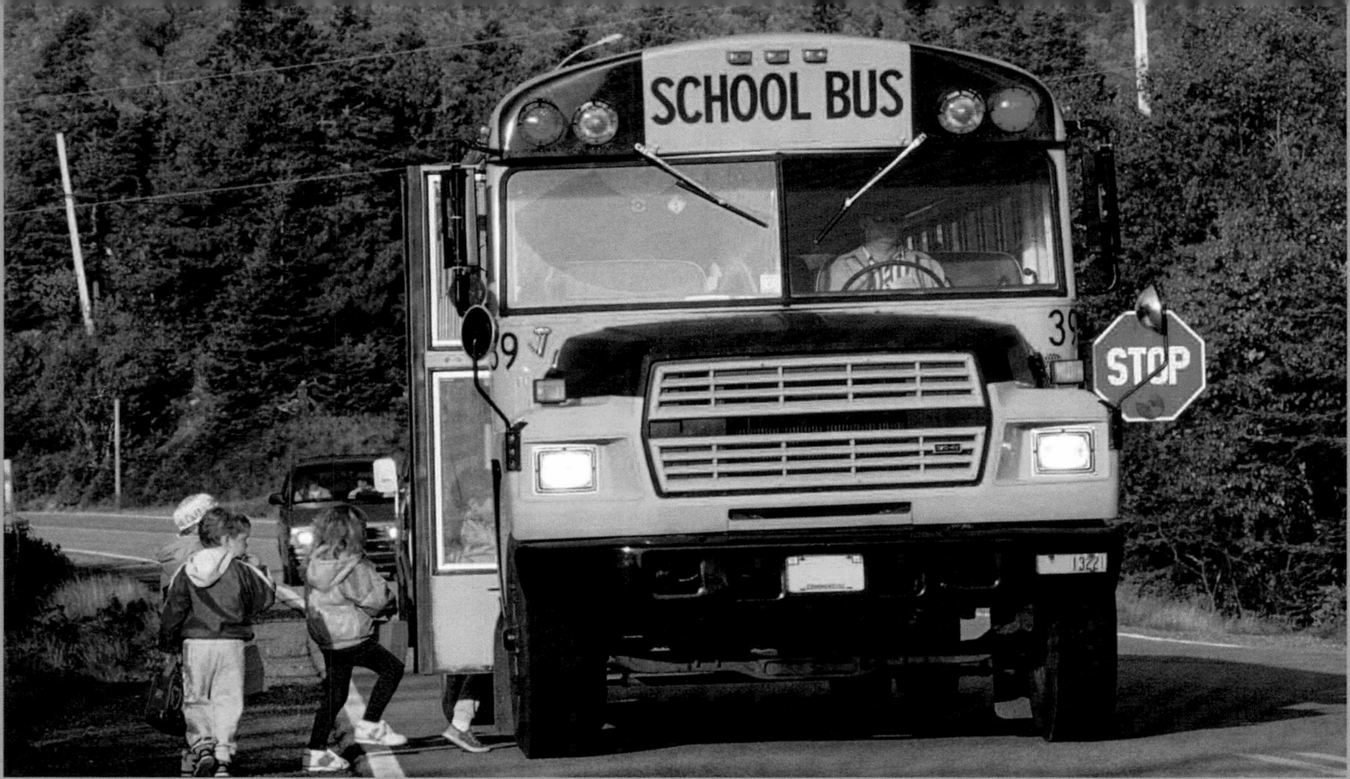


A bus has wheels.

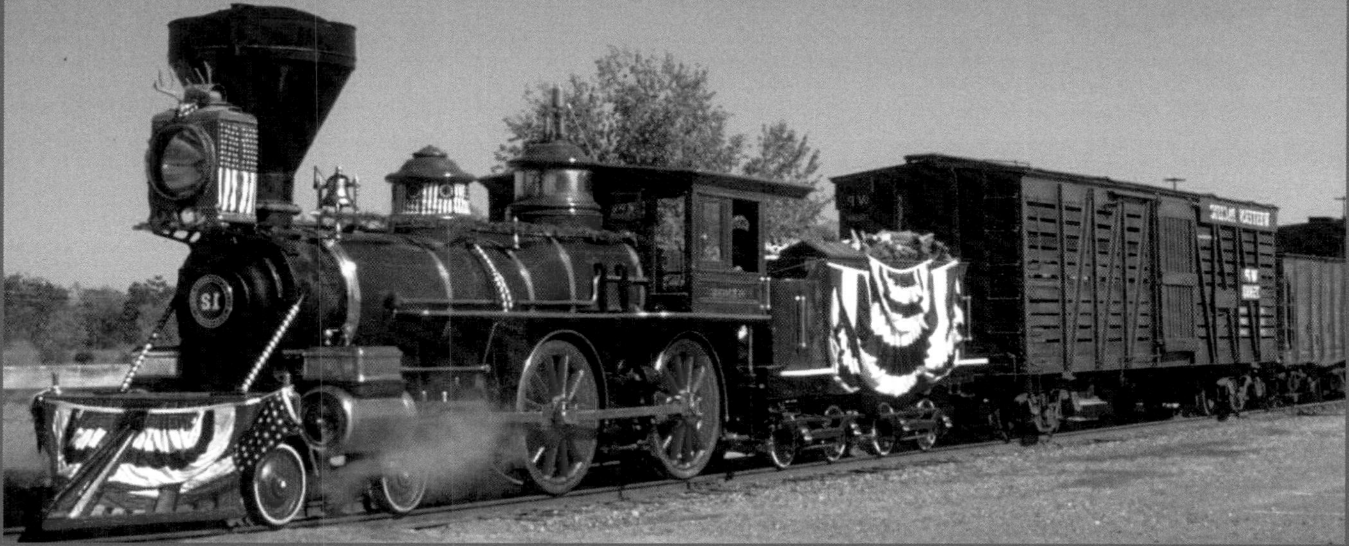

A train has wheels.

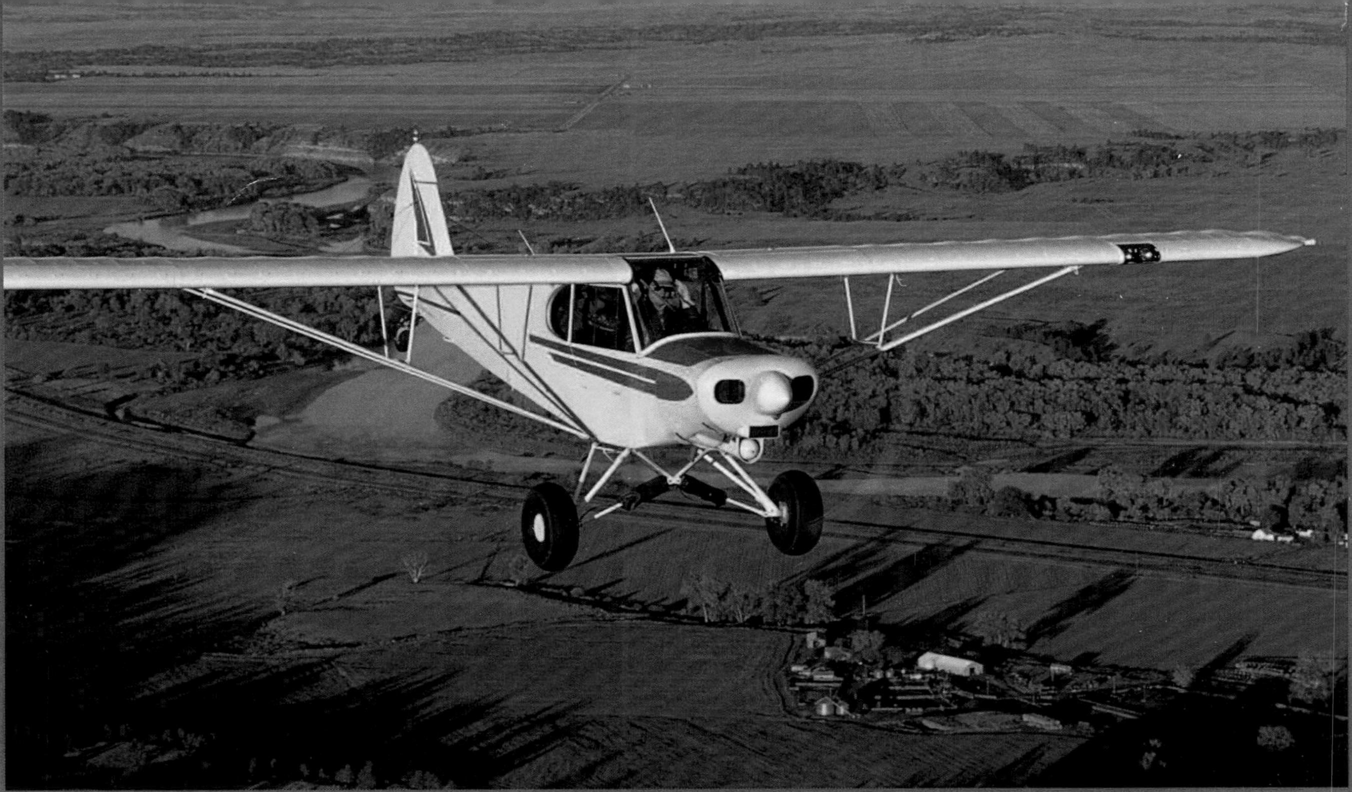

A plane has wheels.